# WHO'S THE PRETTIEST GIRL IN THE WORLD?

Written by **Jamila Avalon**

Illustrated by **Nadia Ronquillo**

# DEDICATION

To my mom, thanks for always reminding me that
I am the prettiest girl in the world!
To my daughter Ava, and every other pretty girl reading this,
never let anyone question what you know to be true.

# ACKNOWLEDGEMENT

To the pretty girls who inspired this book's characters
(and their amazing parents):
Anya, Blake, Kai, Janiyah, Jordyn, and Melina.
## Thank you!

WHO'S
THE PRETTIEST
GIRL
IN THE WORLD?

Who's the prettiest girl
in the world?
The prettiest girl in the world
is you!

And do you know what
all the pretty girls like you do?

They walk and they smile
with their heads held high

whether **bold** or shy.

Who's the prettiest girl in the world?
The prettiest girl in the world is you!
And do you know what all the pretty girls like you do?

They **play** with their toys

And they also **share**

Because
pretty girls are nice and
pretty girls are fair.

Who's the prettiest girl in the world?
The prettiest girl in the world is you!
And do you know what all the pretty girls like you do?

But pretty girls
always give it
another try!

Who's the prettiest girl in the world?
The prettiest girl in the world is you!
And do you know what all the pretty girls like you do?

# Because pretty girls like you can do ANYTHING!

Who's the prettiest girl in the world?
The prettiest girl in the world is you!
And do you know what all the pretty girls like you do?

They soar like a star in every stride

Because what makes a
girl pretty is what's inside

Who's the prettiest girl in the world?
It's me
and me
and us
and you!
16

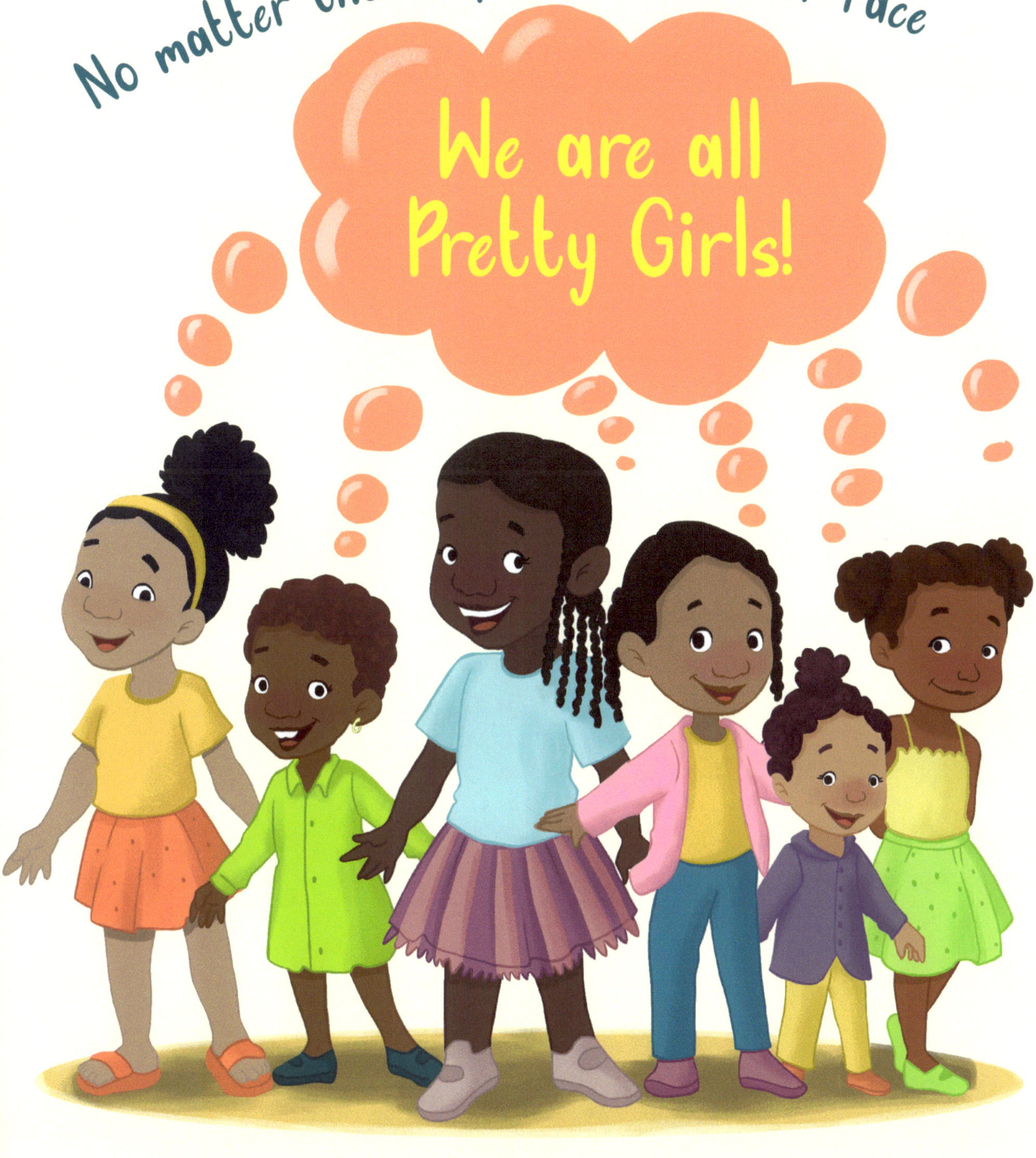

Because pretty is more than what's
on your face

Who's the prettiest girl
in the world?
The prettiest girl
in the world is you!
But I think there's
another word for you.
Yes you are pretty,
but you're this one too.

From your hair to your skin, and all that you do
You're one of a kind, you're perfectly you!

The prettiest girl in the world, that's you.
But the prettiest girl in the world is also

19

Beau

tiful
21